As Koufax Said...

As Koufax Said...

THE 400 BEST THINGS EVER SAID ABOUT HOW TO PLAY BASEBALL

COMPILED BY

Randy Voorhees and Mark Gola

Contemporary Books

Chicago   New York   San Francisco   Lisbon   London   Madrid   Mexico City
Milan   New Delhi   San Juan   Seoul   Singapore   Sydney   Toronto

The *McGraw·Hill* Companies

Library of Congress Cataloging-in-Publication Data

As Koufax said— : the 400 best things ever said about how to play baseball /
  [compiled by] Randy Voorhees and Mark Gola.
        p.   cm.
    Includes bibliographical references and index.
    ISBN 0-07-141014-7
    1. Baseball players—United States—Quotations.   2. Baseball—
United States—Quotations, maxims, etc.   I. Voorhees, Randy.
II. Gola, Mark.

    GV867.3 .A73   2003
    96.357'02—dc17   2003041987

1 2 3 4 5 6 7 8 9 0   LBM/LBM   2 1 0 9 8 7 6 5 4 3

ISBN 0-07-141014-7

Interior illustrations by Dan Krovatin

McGraw-Hill books are available at special quantity discounts to use as premiums
and sales promotions, or for use in corporate training programs. For more
information, please write to the Director of Special Sales, Professional Publishing,
McGraw-Hill, Two Penn Plaza, New York, NY 10121-2298. Or contact your local
bookstore.

This book is printed on acid-free paper.

CONTENTS

PREFACE

This book is for baseball players, baseball coaches, and anyone else searching for a greater understanding of how best to play the game. The book is divided into eight sections: The Game, Practice, Batting, Pitching, Fielding, Baserunning, Managing and Coaching, and Character. Each section contains dozens of quotations—enough so that each part of the game is covered by more than one voice. For example, if you don't like or understand what Maury Wills has to say about base stealing, turn the page and read what Joe Morgan and Lou Brock have to say. You're sure to find something that resonates.

There are many collections of quotations about baseball. *As Koufax Said . . .* , however, is the first book of its kind. All the quotations were selected based on their teaching value. There are no "Yogiisms," "Stengelese," or tales about a player's drinking prowess. We went for the smart quote rather than the cute one.

Everyone who plays or coaches baseball can quote scores of useless things they've heard about the game: "Keep your eye on the ball." "Walks will kill you." "Get in front of the ball." We thought it best to provide players and coaches with some intelligent, useful, and accurate advice (from players at the highest level of the game) instead. You can't go anywhere else to find the collective wisdom and insight of Greg Maddux, Sandy Koufax, Ted Williams, Cal Ripken Jr., John McGraw, and Earl Weaver under the same cover.

Our hope is that your game (or at least your understanding of it) will improve after reading this book. Please notice that some quotations deal with the physical aspects of baseball, others with the mental part. Maybe Lou Piniella can't improve your swing, but he might be able to make you a smarter, more patient hitter. Either way, you'll be better for reading what he has to say.

Certainly, there are hundreds of wonderful quotations that we didn't include in this book. That's either because we didn't find them or because they didn't survive the final editing process. If we've overlooked a favorite gem of yours, please drop us a note c/o Randy Voorhees, 20 New Road, Lambertville, NJ 08530, and we'll try to find a home for it.

ONE

THE GAME

It breaks your heart. It is designed to break your heart.
The game begins in the spring, when everything else
begins again, and it blossoms in the summer, filling the
afternoons and evenings, and then as soon as the chill
rains come, it stops and leaves you to face the fall
alone.

> —*A. Bart Giamatti,*
> *major-league commissioner*
> *(1989)*

Baseball gives every American boy a chance to excel.
Not just to be as good as someone else, but to be better.
This is the nature of man and the name of the game.

> —*Ted Williams,*
> *Hall of Fame player*
> *(1939–1960), manager*

I know that if Lou Gehrig is looking down . . . he isn't
concerned about someone playing one more consecutive
game than he did. He's viewing tonight as another
example of what is good and right about the great
American game.

> —*Cal Ripken Jr.,*
> *major-league player*
> *(1981–2001)*

People ask me what I do in winter when there's no
baseball. I'll tell you what I do. I stare out the window
and wait for spring.

> —*Rogers Hornsby,*
> *Hall of Fame player*
> *(1915–1937), manager*

Baseball gives you every chance to be great. Then it
puts every pressure on you to prove that you haven't got

what it takes. It never takes away that chance, and it never eases up on the pressure.

> —*Joe Garagiola,*
> *major-league player*
> *(1946–1954), broadcaster,*
> *writer*

You see, you spend a good piece of your life gripping a baseball; and in the end it turns out that it was the other way around all the time.

> —*Jim Bouton,*
> *major-league pitcher*
> *(1962–1970, 1978)*

Baseball? It's just a game—as simple as ball and bat, yet as complex as the American spirit it symbolizes. It's a sport, business—and sometimes even religion. Baseball is tradition in flannel knickerbockers. And chagrin in being picked off base. It is dignity in the blue serge of an umpire running the game by rule of thumb. It is humor, holding its sides when an errant puppy eludes two groundskeepers and the fastest outfielder. And pathos dragging itself off the field after being knocked from the box.

> —*Ernie Harwell,*
> *major-league broadcaster,*
> *writer*

. . . a baseball box score is a democratic thing. It doesn't tell how big you are, what church you attend, what color you are, or how your father voted in the last election. It just tells you what kind of baseball player you were on that particular day.

> —*Branch Rickey,*
> *Hall of Fame executive,*
> *player, manager*

Baseball is a kid's game that grown-ups only tend to screw up.

> —*Bob Lemon,*
> *major-league pitcher*
> *(1941–1942, 1946–1958),*
> *manager*

This is a game to be savored, not gulped. There's time to discuss everything between pitches or between innings.

> —*Bill Veeck Sr.,*
> *major-league baseball owner*

The only thing that's certain is that the National Anthem is played before every game.

> —*Rick Monday,*
> *major-league player*
> *(1966–1984)*

Balance is the first lesson I should teach a beginner. To be sure, no one taught me, but I consider it the basis of successful work in any one of the three departments: batting, fielding, and baserunning.

> —*Max Carey,*
> *major-league player*
> *(1910–1929), manager*

The game of baseball is made up of many little things. If we do all the little things right, then we'll never have a big thing to worry about.

> —*Cal Ripken Sr.,*
> *major-league manager,*
> *coach (1976–1986, 1989–1992)*

Baseball is a lot like life. The line drives are caught, the squibblers go for base hits. It's an unfair game.

>   —*Rod Kanehl,*
>   *major-league player*
>   *(1962–1964)*

Baseball is like church. Many attend, but few understand.

>   —*Wes Westrum,*
>   *major-league player*
>   *(1947–1957), manager*

ABOVE THE SHOULDERS

I have never known a day when I didn't learn something new about this game.

>   —*Connie Mack,*
>   *major-league manager*
>   *(1894–1896, 1901–1950)*

This game is played with confidence because this game is played with your head. Most people have the physical ability to play this game. To excel in it, I think it's in your head.

> —*Ron Darling,*
> *major-league pitcher*
> *(1983–1995)*

Baseball requires a player who is keen witted and intelligent. That type of mind, which is not only active but original, always trying something new, is the highest type of baseball mind.

> —*Dasher Troy,*
> *major-league player*
> *(1883–1885)*

I think *why* is a wonderful word.

> —*Ted Williams*

The game is the count.

> —*Bob Welch,*
> *major-league pitcher*
> *(1978–1994)*

Stay within yourself is baseball's first commandment.
. . . A player's reach should not exceed his grasp.

> —*George Will,*
> *author, baseball historian*

The less time you spend thinking about it, the less
trouble you'll get into. I think the game's more
intelligent than most of the guys playing it.

> —*Jeff Russell,*
> *major-league pitcher*
> *(1983–1996)*

I've always said that in baseball, you can't try too hard.
You have to do everything easy.

> —*George Brett,*
> *Hall of Fame player*
> *(1973–1993)*

I think about baseball when I wake up in the morning.
I think about it all day. And I dream about it at night.
The only time I don't think about it is when I'm
playing it.

> —*Carl Yastrzemski,*
> *major-league player*
> *(1961–1983)*

Everything we do in baseball we do out in front: We catch the ball out in front, we throw the ball out in front, and we hit the ball out in front. This is so the eyes can relay information to the fastest computer in the world—the human brain—and then that computer can get the rest of the body in the right place.

—Cal Ripken Sr.

FOR THE LOVE OF THE GAME

I like to play happy. Baseball is a fun game, and I love it.

—Willie Mays,
Hall of Fame player
(1951–1973)

Baseball is not pressure. Pressure is when you're seven years old, and you don't have food to eat. So when you've come from nowhere and have all that I have now, I sleep like a baby every night.

—Sammy Sosa,
major-league player
(1989–present)

The umpire says "Play ball," not "Work ball."

> *—Willie Stargell,*
> *Hall of Fame player*
> *(1962–1982)*

This is what God chose me to do. He sent me here to play baseball.

> *—Roberto Alomar,*
> *major-league player*
> *(1988–present)*

It's difficult for me to explain how much I love baseball. We've been together for 22 years. It was a love affair.

> *—Willie Mays*

TWO

PRACTICE

When you're through learning, you're through.

—Vern Law,
major-league pitcher
(1950–1951, 1954–1967)

Giving myself wholeheartedly to workouts was no guarantee of success in the win-loss column. It did, however, rule out laziness and bad work habits as excuses.

—Orel Hershiser,
major-league pitcher
(1983–2000), coach

If you're not practicing, somebody else is, somewhere, and he'll be ready to take your job.

> —Brooks Robinson,
> Hall of Fame player
> (1955–1977)

This is not an easy game. To be a champion, you have to invest a little extra.

> —Pete Rose,
> major-leaguer player
> (1963–1986),
> manager (1984–1989)

A baseball workout doesn't have to be complicated. You want to strengthen your arm? Throw the ball. Want to strengthen your legs? Run. The best exercises are throwing a ball, hitting a ball, and catching a ball.

> —Cal Ripken Sr.

People who write about spring training not being necessary have never tried to throw a baseball.

> —Sandy Koufax,
> Hall of Fame pitcher
> (1955–1966)

Have you ever noticed how the pepper hitter always gets a piece of the ball? You can never fool him. Throw him a curveball, fastball, slider, or change-of-pace, and he'll have no problem. I've been in pepper games where pro pitchers are throwing nearly their best stuff and the hitter always gets a piece of the ball. We need to ask ourselves why. The answer is obvious. Because he doesn't try to hit the ball out in front of the plate. He waits for the ball to come to him and makes square, center-field contact over the plate.

—Mike Schmidt,
Hall of Fame player
(1972–1989)

You can't practice enough the transfer of the ball from glove to hand. You have to keep doing it until reaching in and grabbing that ball across the seams becomes second nature. Practice this even when you're having a simple catch.

—Johnny Bench,
Hall of Fame player
(1967–1983)

That one exhibition season, John Sain must have kept me after practice 15 times and he threw me nothing but curveballs—slow curves, biting curves, curves in the dirt, changing speeds on curves. Once I'd seen enough of the damn things, I began to get a feel for them. I learned to lay back on that pitch and how to look for it, how to rip it or take it to the opposite field. I never had a better feeling than when I started stroking them around the yard off of old John Sain.

> —*Whitey Herzog,*
> *major-league player*
> *(1956–1963),*
> *manager (1973–1990)*

You must come to practice every day with a definite goal in mind. You don't have to spend hours on your weaknesses, just as long as you recognize them as weaknesses and are devoted to turning a negative into a positive.

> —*Rod Carew,*
> *Hall of Fame player*
> *(1967–1985)*

Practice doesn't make perfect, because you can practice bad habits and never get any better. . . . You play like you practice, and if you practice correctly, you'll play correctly.

> —*Cal Ripken Sr.*

In my senior year of high school, I won six games and lost five. Even at USC [University of Southern California], I had to work hard just to be a starter. Pitching has always been hard work for me.

> —*Tom Seaver,*
> *Hall of Fame pitcher*
> *(1967–1986)*

A guy doesn't get in the batting cage often enough and doesn't stay there long enough. You see it even in the Little Leagues. With all the regimentation they get, and all the emphasis on playing games instead of practicing, a kid isn't afforded the time he needs in the batting cage.

> —*Ted Williams*

PRACTICE TO A TEE

In many respects, the batting tee is the Rodney Dangerfield of baseball equipment: It doesn't get any respect. But it does from Rod Carew. Kids laugh at the batting tee as being elementary. But that's how you learn, how you teach—by breaking hitting down to its simplest, most fundamental form.

> —*Rod Carew*

There are a lot of expensive machines on the market to
help you become a better hitter. I've got most of them
because the manufacturers send them to me to try out.
Some of them aren't bad. But I know about a device
you can buy for about $15 that will help you learn a lot.
It's called a batting tee.

> —*Tony Gwynn,*
> *major-league player*
> *(1982–2001), college coach*

Hitting balls off the tee is an important part of
warming up before the game. I imagine that I'm hitting
off David Wells or Pedro Martinez when I swing
through smacking the ball to the right, center, and left.
It can be a little monotonous practicing my swing over
and over again, but it pays off in the long run.

> —*Derek Jeter,*
> *major-league player*
> *(1995–present)*

THREE

BATTING

A great hitter isn't born, he's made. He's made out of practice, fault correction, and confidence.

—*Rogers Hornsby*

Fielding is good and so is baserunning, but the manager will overlook a lot of faults in the player who bats .375.

—*Zack Wheat,*
major-league player
(1909–1927)

What I have learned about batting nobody taught me. I
had to dig it out for myself.

> —*George Sisler,*
> *Hall of Fame player*
> *(1915–1922, 1924–1930)*

All good balls to hit are strikes, though not all strikes
are good balls to hit.

> —*Dave Winfield,*
> *major-league player*
> *(1973–1988, 1990–1995)*

The secret of good batting, in my opinion, is to hit
only good balls.

> —*Rogers Hornsby*

I swing big and I miss big.

> —*Babe Ruth,*
> *Hall of Fame player*
> *(1914–1935)*

Every man has his natural style and should follow it. I have my style, and I couldn't hit if I tried to copy somebody else.

> —*Joe Jackson,*
> *major-league player*
> *(1908–1920)*

Hitting is a lot more than just picking up a bat and swinging it. You've got to be observant, evaluate the situation, know the pitcher and his tendencies, and know yourself. If you want to be successful, you have to become a student.

> —*Paul O'Neill,*
> *major-league player*
> *(1985–2001)*

If you play for 10 years in the major leagues and have 7,000 at-bats and 2,000 hits, you have had a pretty fair career, but you've gone 0-for-5,000.

> —*Reggie Jackson,*
> *Hall of Fame player*
> *(1967–1987)*

A relaxed hitter is a good hitter. You are the quickest when you're relaxed.

> —*Bobby Bonds,*
> *major-league player*
> *(1968–1981), coach*

A crack shot can hit a bird on the wing because his eye and his finger on the trigger act together. The amateur hunter can see the bird as well as the expert, but his finger on the trigger is perhaps a fraction of a second late. The good batter is like the good marksman. His wrists and his shoulders act with the eye.

> —*Jake Daubert,*
> *major-league player*
> *(1910–1924)*

You want to know what the best hitters can do? They can hit deep in the count. That's the one thing that separates the great hitters from good hitters.

> —*Lou Piniella,*
> *major-league player,*
> *manager (1986–present)*

HITTER VERSUS PITCHER

I have said that a good hitter can hit a pitch that is over the plate three times better than a great hitter with a questionable ball in a tough spot. Pitchers still make enough mistakes to give you some in your happy zone. But the greatest living hitter can't hit bad balls good.

—Ted Williams

Every great batter works on the theory that the pitcher is more afraid of him than he is of the pitcher.

—Ty Cobb,
Hall of Fame player
(1905–1928), manager

I firmly believe that a lot of at-bats are determined before you get in the box. I firmly believe you can empower a pitcher at times by your body language and how you react to certain situations. . . . Don't let them see you sweat. Don't let them think you're bothered. . . .

—Clint Hurdle,
major-league player
(1977–1987),
manager, coach

When you're not comfortable, you find yourself
thinking about what he's [the pitcher's] trying to do to
you. When I hit the best, I'm comfortable and I don't
care what they're going to throw.

          —George Brett

The smart pitchers today can capitalize on the hitter's
fondness for home runs. . . . Pitchers couldn't get away
with that as often when I pitched, but today's can. The
hitters make it easier, even those who don't have the
strength to be home run hitters.

          —Bob Feller,
           Hall of Fame pitcher
           (1936–1941, 1945–1956)

Now when I was up there, I would know what I was
going to do, but I couldn't tell you what the pitcher was
going to do.

          —Andy High,
           major-league player
           (1922–1934)

You don't always *make* an out. Sometimes the pitcher
gets you out.

          —Carl Yastrzemski

If you want to be a consistent hitter, you've got to know the strike zone. Swinging at strikes not only increases your chances to hit the ball well and reach first base, but it also makes the pitcher work harder.

> —Lenny Dykstra,
> major-league player
> (1985–1996)

When I was a pitcher myself, I always figured that when I had the batters swinging I had them beat. It's the waiting batter that worries a pitcher. Then you have to keep on getting the ball over the plate. That is a continual strain on a pitcher and the very thing he likes least of all.

> —George Sisler

You must learn to make that first time up a key time by striving to find out as much about a pitcher as possible, and you do that by making him pitch. It's simple arithmetic: You figure to face a pitcher at least three to four times in a game. The more information you log the first time up, the better your chances the next three. The more you make him pitch, the more information you get.

> —Ted Williams

When the pitcher is in a tough spot, he will do his best to get you to go for bad balls. But always remember, a walk is as good as a hit.

> —*Joe DiMaggio,*
> *Hall of Fame player*
> *(1936–1942, 1946–1951)*

AN APPROACH AT THE PLATE

I never go up to the plate without a plan. The plan, however, depends on what you've seen from the pitcher, what his tendencies are, how you're feeling that day, what the game situation is, and what he's most likely to throw at that point in time.

> —*Will Clark,*
> *major-league player*
> *(1986–2000)*

When I'm on deck, I'm just thinking about seeing the baseball, and then seeing myself hit the ball hard.

> —*Mark McGwire,*
> *major-league player*
> *(1986–2001)*

I am relaxed, confident, and always try to hit the ball where it's pitched, from foul line to foul line.

> —*Mark Grace,*
> *major-league player*
> *(1988–present)*

I would occasionally go to a heavier bat against soft-throwing left-handers. I knew I didn't have to be quite as quick against them, and the bat's additional mass helped me drive the ball.

> —*Joe Morgan,*
> *Hall of Fame player*
> *(1963–1984), broadcaster*

The best thought process is to hit the ball back through the middle, right back at the pitcher. That way, an outside strike and the inside strike become a reaction.

> —*Mike Lieberthal,*
> *major-league player*
> *(1994–present)*

I hated to be early on a pitch because everything is wrong then—I wasn't waiting, I was probably fooled, I was too far in front to hit the ball with authority. If I was behind a little, it didn't hurt as much because if

you are quick with the bat—and I preach quickness—
you'll do all right.

> —*Ted Williams*

If all they give you is lemons, then make lemonade.
Take the walk to first base.

> —*Alex Rodriguez,*
> *major-league player*
> *(1994–present)*

Why look for a pitch you know you can't hit? Look for
what you *can* hit, in case you get it.

> —*Ron Fairly,*
> *major-league player*
> *(1958–1978)*

A lot of hitters change their swing when they get
behind in the count. When they get two strikes on
them, they choke up on the bat and shorten their
swing—they're just going to try to meet the ball. I say,
why? . . . If I have two strikes on me, that isn't going to
change anything. I've still got one more opportunity to
hit the ball. Therefore, I'm going up there and do
things the way I want to do them.

> —*Tony Gwynn*

I had the greatest day of my career [after hitting four home runs]. I probably will never have another one like it again. If I'd gone up again, I might have pressed— gone for the home run. And when you press, you're dead. Seldom have I ever really tried to hit a home run and got it.

—*Willie Mays*

When I got two hits in a game, I came up wanting a third. If I got a third, I had to get a fourth. I never knew when I might go 0-for-4, so I was always hungry for more base hits.

—*Stan Musial,*
Hall of Fame player
(1941–1963)

I used to watch every pitch right into the catcher's mitt when I didn't swing. I started doing that when I was seven or eight years old. It gives you a longer look when you're taking a pitch. You track it all the way, right to the catcher's mitt. It's good practice for making you stay on the ball longer and helping you wait longer.

—*Wade Boggs,*
major-league player
(1982–1999)

CONFIDENCE

Every time I stepped up to the plate with a bat in my hands, I felt sorry for them [the pitchers].

—Rogers Hornsby

Confidence is everything.

—Joe Morgan

You've got to have the mentality that you are going to make somebody pay when you're at bat.

—Mo Vaughn,
major-league player
(1991–present)

If you hit the ball hard, you've done your job. What happens after that is beyond your control. This game is fixed on results, but if you focus on statistics, you can lose your confidence and create a slump in your mind.

—Travis Lee,
major-league player
(1998–present)

You can't be afraid of the baseball. You've got to attack the baseball.

> —*Jay Bell,*
>   *major-league player*
>   *(1986–present)*

Confidence is as important to hitting a baseball as the bat you're holding in your hands.

> —*Will Clark*

HIT IT WHERE IT'S PITCHED

I can step into any pitch and not get handcuffed by an inside strike. I can still reach anything on the outside corner and hit it hard to the opposite field. Middle of the plate and in, I can go long-ball. But the same reflexes that allow me to do that—I have to count on them to keep me from being beaned, because I might step into a fastball coming at my head.

> —*Mike Schmidt*

Gear yourself to hit the ball away and let the inside
pitches take care of themselves.

> —*Charlie Lau,*
> *major-league player, coach*
> *(1969–1983)*

One of the keys to hitting the outside strike is when to
attack it. You don't necessarily have to swing at it.
That's the pitcher's pitch. Balls down the middle and on
the inside part of the plate is where hitters have most
success. Obviously, with two strikes you have to
protect, but until then, try to get something better
to hit.

> —*Jay Bell*

To hit the ball to the opposite field, you've got to let
the ball travel back. It's that plain and simple.

> —*Mike Lieberthal*

If you ask most hitters which ball is easiest to hit,
they're going to say the ball inside—the fastball inside,
the reaction pitch. So they go up there looking for it,
and to me, that's a problem. If you are looking for the
ball inside, you're going to have trouble adjusting to the
ball outside.

> —*Tony Gwynn*

HITTING OFF-SPEED PITCHES

The most important element to hitting a breaking ball
is letting it get to you.

—Scott Rolen,
major-league player
(1996–present)

A pretty good rule of thumb for amateur hitters is not
to swing at a breaking ball until you are forced to with
two strikes.

—Mike Schmidt

It's easier to hit a breaking ball than a fastball, because
you get more time to look at it.

—Tony Gwynn

There are two theories on hitting the knuckleball.
Unfortunately, neither of them work.

—Charlie Lau

SWING MECHANICS

Hitting is such a complex and difficult process that anxiety and frustration will set in quickly unless you have some foundation of instruction to build on. Simply put, if you ignore any of those fundamentals of hitting, the entire action falls apart.

> —*Jerry Kindall,*
> *college coach*

You have to learn the basic fundamentals of the swing and go from there. You don't set out to become Mark McGwire and start by imitating his swing. Chances are, you're not going to become Mark McGwire. There is only one of him. Start simple and build on your personal strengths.

> —*Doug Glanville,*
> *major-league player*
> *(1996–present)*

Good hitting is like highway construction: closed shoulders.

> —*George Kissell,*
> *major-league coach*
> *(1969–1975)*

PRE-SWING

The most important thing about finding your grip is to remove tension. Anything you can do to take tension away helps, because tension destroys a hitter.

—Charlie Lau

Choking up gave me better bat control. I would slide my hands an inch or two above the knob of the bat. Many people believe that choke hitters can't generate power, but Ted Williams choked up and he has over 500 career home runs on his resume.

—Joe Morgan

I've seen many a fellow who chased himself right back to the minor leagues because he wouldn't choke up on his bat.

*—Smokey Joe Wood,
major-league pitcher
(1908–1922)*

A lot of young players believe choking up isn't manly or is a sign of weak hitting. Nonsense. Choking up is a smart move that shortens and lightens the bat. Choking up makes it easier for you to guide your bat to the ball.

—Wade Boggs

Whenever I brought my arms too close to my body, I
tended to upper-cut the ball. The result? Too many fly-
ball outs. That habit was tough to break. The late
Nellie Fox, a Hall of Fame second baseman and a
player/coach when I played with the Houston Astros,
suggested that I flap my elbows whenever I was at the
plate as a reminder to keep my arms away from my
torso. I was only supposed to do this for a few days,
but the "chicken flap" became part of my hitting
routine. It kept my elbows out and got me ready to hit.

—*Joe Morgan*

I hold my shoulders high when I swing at the ball. The
batter is more likely to hit true if the bat moves
parallel.

—*Tris Speaker,*
Hall of Fame player
(1907–1928)

I don't know of any great hitters who aren't short
striders.

—*Branch Rickey*

Exactly when you lift your foot and take your stride
varies, depending on the kind of pitchers you're facing.
If it's Tom Candiotti, who throws a real slow

knuckleball, it doesn't make any sense to sit up there and start going into your routine when he gets to the release point because the ball isn't coming to you for a while. But with pitchers like John Smoltz or Randy Johnson, guys who throw real hard, maybe you start just a hair before they get to the release point.

> —*Tony Gwynn*

If you don't get your stride foot down in time, you've got no foundation.

> —*Alex Rodriguez*

I believe in movement. You cannot do anything from a dead standstill. All the good hitters I've seen move. You have to have rhythm. . . .

> —*Dusty Baker,*
> *major-league player*
> *(1968–1986), manager*
> *(1993–present)*

Although it isn't always obvious, good hitters always have some kind of movement in the stance. They're like a car with its engine idling, just before you pop the clutch. They can thus be quicker and shift their weight more effectively than someone who stands dead still.

> —*Charlie Lau*

It's only a hitch when you're in a slump. When you're hittin' the ball, it's called rhythm.

> —*Eddie Mathews,*
> *Hall of Fame player*
> *(1952–1968)*

It's very important to get something moving back before you start your swing forward. In our business, it's called loading and it's just like a prize fighter loading to throw a punch. By moving back first, you'll generate more power.

> —*Will Clark*

If you look at all the good hitters, what's important is not so much where the bat starts in the stance, it's what position it's in the moment before it starts to come forward.

> —*Tony Gwynn*

It's hard to see with the naked eye, but no matter where the bat is when they're in their stance, all good hitters have it in the launching position when their front foot completes the stride. They all step to swing. They never combine the two motions.

> —*Charlie Lau*

You're making the pitcher faster than he really is when the head travels forward a lot. And any time the body moves, the eyes move. When the eyes move, the ball takes a bad hop on the way in.

> —*Richie Zisk,*
> *major-league player*
> *(1971–1983)*

SWING

It don't mean a thing if you ain't got that swing.

> —*Tony Oliva,*
> *major-league player*
> *(1962–1976), coach*

I don't believe in the hitter creating weight shift. I think the bat should transfer the weight to the front side. The weight follows the bat as opposed to the weight shifting in front of the barrel.

> —*Hal McRae,*
> *major-league player*
> *(1968, 1970–1987),*
> *manager, coach*

Anyone who thinks long swings produce long hits is preaching inaccurate information. Be short and explode through the ball. A short swing means quickness, and you've got to be quick in this game.

—Mark McGwire

It's not a wrist roll. It's a wrist snap. If you do it correctly, it keeps the barrel through the hitting zone without changing its path and without lifting over the ball and creating topspin.

—Dave Gallagher,
major-league player
(1987–1995), college coach

You know, in boxing, when you hit a man, your fist generally stops right there, but it is possible to hit a man so hard that your fist doesn't stop. When I carry through with the bat, it is for the same reason.

—Babe Ruth

When you try to hit the ball for power, your swing gets too long. The best thing to do is stay back, see the ball, and then explode through the ball.

> —*Dante Bichette,*
> *major-league player*
> *(1988–2002)*

The top hand finishes off what the bottom hand starts.

> —*Frank Robinson,*
> *Hall of Fame player*
> *(1956–1976), manager*

The farther outside the ball is, the longer you wait.

> —*Rod Carew*

The longer you can look at a pitch, the better your chances of hitting it.

> —*Tony Gwynn*

One mistake hitters make is that they fail to trust their hands. They think the pitcher is throwing harder than he is and fly open prematurely. Trust your hands, see the ball first, and then react to its location.

> —*Mike Lieberthal*

If I could tell Little League and other young players only one thing that would improve their hitting, it would be this: Your head goes down when you swing. At the moment of contact . . . your head should be down. . . .

—Charlie Lau

SLUMPS

Most slumps are like the common cold. They last two weeks no matter what you do.

> *—Terry Kennedy,*
> *major-league player*
> *(1978–1991)*

If I'm hitting, I can hit anyone. If not, my 12-year-old son can get me out.

—Willie Stargell

The most important thing is knowing *why* you made an out.

> *—Rusty Staub,*
> *major-league player*
> *(1963–1985)*

If a hitter isn't getting jammed from time to time, he's not waiting on the ball. He's pulling out his front side.

—*Al Kaline,*
Hall of Fame player
(1953–1974)

I have always maintained that the best remedy for a batting slump is two wads of cotton. One for each ear.

—*Bill Veeck Sr.*

If it works, stick with it. Sometimes coaches like to try to make changes for the sake of change. Stick with what feels comfortable.

—*Travis Lee*

When you're struggling at the plate, any one of several things can pull you out of it. Sometimes extra batting practice, sometimes a day off, and sometimes it's a flare hit that will make you feel as if things are about to turn your way. It's all about finding whatever it takes to regain your confidence at the plate.

—*Jay Bell*

When I've gotten into trouble, it's often because I'm not aggressive enough. I take too many pitches.

> —*John Olerud,*
> *major-league player*
> *(1989–present)*

When I struggle, I realize that I'm not seeing the ball. To fix the problem, I don't worry about where my hands are, how my feet are set up, or where my weight is. I concentrate on seeing the ball and hitting it right back up the middle.

> —*Scott Rolen*

You decide you'll wait for your pitch. Then as the ball starts toward the plate, you think about your stance. And then you think about your swing. And then you realize that the ball that went past you for a strike was your pitch.

> —*Bobby Murcer,*
> *major-league player*
> *(1965–1983)*

SITUATIONAL HITTING

One of the greatest fallacies in baseball is the theory
that a left-handed batter cannot hit left-handed
pitching. . . . Players who accept [this] theory at its face
value believe they cannot hit certain types of pitching.
By working the groove of this idea in a player's mind,
his confidence is shaken and he fails to hit. Besides, the
manager will not give him the chance to practice
against left-handers, and this in itself adds to his
batting weakness.

—Rogers Hornsby

A good leadoff hitter is a pain in the ass to pitchers.

—Richie Ashburn,
Hall of Fame player
(1948–1962), broadcaster

There is only one legitimate trick to pinch-hitting, and
that's knowing the pitcher's best pitch when the count
is 3-and-2. All the rest is a crapshoot.

—Earl Weaver,
major-league manager
(1968–1986)

No matter how fast the ball may break, your eye is quicker than the ball and so is the end of the bat.

—*Rogers Hornsby*

If I wasn't expected to drive the ball out of the lot every time I come up there to the plate, I'd change my batting form tomorrow. I'd copy Cobb's style in every single thing he does.

—*Babe Ruth*

Walks aren't a sign of weak hitting—they're a sign of smart hitting and team hitting. . . . Walks minimize outs, set up or sustain rallies, and win games. A walk may not always be as good as a hit, but walks create base runners and base runners score runs.

—*Wade Boggs*

The key to making good contact as a bunter is the exact opposite of what we teach for making good contact as a hitter. In hitting, the action we initiate thrusts the head of the bat toward the ball. In bunting, we want to let the ball come toward the bat. A big mistake bad bunters make is trying to jab the bat at the ball. Once you've moved your bat into the bunting zone, the only time the bat, or any part of your body,

should move is when the ball actually makes contact
with the bat.

—*Rod Carew*

Beating out a bunt isn't just as good as a hit, it *is* a hit.

—*Wade Boggs*

The main reason the average bunter fails is that he
refuses to give himself up. Instead of bunting just to
advance the base runner, the batter bunts with the idea
in mind of beating it out for a base hit, bunting and
running at the same time.

—*Joe DiMaggio*

Work on bat control. There is always a place on any
team for a guy who can handle the bat.

> —*Harry Walker,*
> *major-league player*
> *(1940–1955), manager, coach*

I've always believed that the most important aspect of
hitting is driving in runs. Runs batted in are more
important than batting average, more important than

home runs, more important than anything. That's what wins ball games. . . .

> —*Hank Greenberg,*
> *Hall of Fame player*
> *(1930, 1933–1941, 1945–1947)*

Ninety-five percent of fly balls are certain outs. Ground balls get through the infield for hits, move the runners up, and put pressure on infielders. They are always potentially productive. More runs are knocked in with ground balls than fly balls.

> —*Mike Schmidt*

Your bat is your life. It's your weapon. You don't want to go into battle with anything that feels less than perfect.

> —*Lou Brock,*
> *Hall of Fame player*
> *(1961–1979)*

FOUR

PITCHING

A guy who throws what he intends to throw—that's the definition of a good pitcher.

—Sandy Koufax

The man with the ball is responsible for what happens.

—Branch Rickey

I always felt the pitcher had the advantage. It's like serving in tennis.

—Allie Reynolds,
major-league pitcher
(1942–1954)

The person holding the ball obviously has an advantage, and I do believe that good pitching will beat good hitting. But remember, that doesn't necessarily mean that good hitters won't hit good pitching.

—*Dan Plesac,*
major-league pitcher
(1986–2002)

It seems like one of the requirements for pitching now is "What's his size?" Really, what you need to do to be a successful pitcher are only two things: Locate your fastball and change speeds. It's definitely an advantage to be big. But it's not a disadvantage to be small.

—*Greg Maddux,*
major-league pitcher
(1986–present)

MIND GAMES

When you understand yourself more as a pitcher, it's easier to pitch. . . . Hitters have been the same since I came up. You've got some righties; you've got some lefties; you've got some fastball hitters; you've got some guys that'll steal bases, guys that hit homers. They just have a different name on their back. That's why I think understanding *yourself* makes it easier.

—*Greg Maddux*

Never let the failure of your last pitch affect the success of your next one.

—*Nolan Ryan,*
Hall of Fame pitcher
(1966, 1968–1993)

Only three or four outs directly affect the outcome of any given game. Stated another way, a game may ride on just three or four pitches that the pitcher must choose carefully and throw with accuracy.

—*Tom Seaver*

If they get a hit, I'm throwing a one-hitter. If they get a walk, it's my last walk. I deal with perfection to the point that is logical to conceive it. History is history. The future is perfect.

—*Orel Hershiser*

We always think about a "closer" as someone who finishes a game. A good starting pitcher closes nine times—once an inning.

> —*Jim Lefebvre,*
> *major-league player*
> *(1965–1972), manager, coach*

[Steve] Carlton used to go into a trancelike state in the pen before he would warm up and I used to think he was just taking a nap. But what he was doing was visualizing the outside lane and the inside lane of the plate under the theory that thought precedes action and you keep the ball away from the fat part of the bat.

> —*Tim McCarver,*
> *major-league player*
> *(1959–1980), broadcaster*

All I can see is the catcher's glove when I'm going good.

> —*Dan Schatzeder,*
> *major-league pitcher*
> *(1977–1991)*

[Nolan] Ryan said there are things I can and can't do on days I pitch. He said I can't control the weather, the umpires, or the emotional state of the other team. But I can control one thing. I can be better prepared than the hitters I face that day.

—Curt Schilling,
major-league pitcher
(1988–present)

Numbers are in the past, and they don't help me get anyone out. I just know what they can do when they get into your mind and make you think things you don't need to think.

—Mark Davis,
major-league pitcher
(1980–1981, 1983–1994, 1997)

The best pitch you can throw is a comfortable pitch, the pitch that you believe in, even if it's the wrong pitch.

—Greg Maddux

I have learned not to trust my stuff in the bullpen as a guide to how well I will do in a game. If you are a positive-minded competitor, your warm-up time is certainly a hopeful time, but don't be overly influenced by what happens in the bullpen. Warming up is when you establish your delivery, making sure it is regular and rhythmic with each pitch.

—Tom Seaver

If we're going bad, [Johnny] Sain would tell us to look
at our old scrapbooks.

> —*Goose Gossage,*
> *major-league pitcher*
> *(1972–1994)*

Pitching is really just an internal struggle between the
pitcher and his stuff. If my curveball is breaking and
I'm throwing it where I want, the batter is irrelevant.

> —*Steve Stone,*
> *major-league pitcher*
> *(1971–1981), broadcaster*

I can control the pitches I make, how I handle my
mechanics, how I control my frame of mind. [It]
benefited me most . . . when I realized that I can't
control what happens outside of my pitching.

> —*Greg Maddux*

A lot of people have asked me how I could stand the
pressure of relief pitching. Well, to me, I didn't feel like
I had pressure. I had eight guys to help me. The batter
had nobody.

> —*Roy Face,*
> *major-league pitcher*
> *(1953–1969)*

A victory used to give me pleasure, then a well-pitched inning, and now I get satisfaction from just one or two pitches a game.

—Tom Seaver

I think too much on the mound sometimes, and I get brain cramps.

—Britt Burns,
major-league pitcher
(1978–1985)

The good Lord was good to me. He gave me a good body, a strong right arm, and a weak mind.

—Dizzy Dean,
Hall of Fame pitcher
(1930–1947)

MOUND PRESENCE

Neither his fastball nor his curve is remarkable. Indeed they are only ordinary, but there is something about [Christy] Mathewson, though—his bearing, his

manner—that gives you the impression that you are
going up against Gibraltar.

> —*Eddie Collins,*
> *major-league player*
> *(1906–1930)*

My approach entering a game is this: I'm gonna beat
you. I'm coming after you and here it comes.

> —*Billy Wagner,*
> *major-league pitcher*
> *(1995–present)*

Work fast, throw strikes, change speeds.

> —*Ray Miller,*
> *major-league manager, coach*
> *(1978–1997)*

I concede nothing. . . . Nothing will happen until I
throw the ball, and I won't give in on any pitch.

> —*Curt Schilling*

You're supposed to win when you have all your pitches
going for you. You haven't become a good pitcher until
you can win when you don't have anything.

> —*Sandy Koufax*

I don't have Nolan Ryan's fastball and I don't have Steve
Carlton's slider or Mario Soto's change-up, but when I
go to the mound, the one thing I usually take with me
is a good attitude.

> —*Rick Sutcliffe,*
> *major-league pitcher*
> *(1976, 1978–1994),*
> *broadcaster*

You had better understand that you are going to make
some bad pitches along the way. That's just the way it
is. . . . If you make a pitch *aggressively*, you have a
much better chance of getting away with it. However,
if you make a pitch tentatively or cautiously, that's
when you get nailed.

> —*Kevin Brown,*
> *major-league pitcher*
> *(1986, 1988–present)*

When pitchers are offensive, the batters become
defensive.

> —*Ray Miller*

You do everything you can to get an edge, but don't let
some of these pitchers fool you with the way they talk.
We're not that smart out there. A good amount of the

time we just go at the hitter with what we've got and
try to beat them.

>*—Jesse Orosco,*
>*major-league pitcher*
>*(1979–present)*

It helps if the hitter thinks you're a little crazy.

>*—Nolan Ryan*

Once I got mad, I was totally useless.

>*—Al Hrabosky,*
>*major-league pitcher*
>*(1970–1982)*

LOCATION

You gotta keep the ball off the fat part of the bat.

>*—Satchel Paige,*
>*Hall of Fame pitcher*
>*(1948–1953, 1965)*

The wildest pitch is not necessarily the one that goes back to the screen. It can also be the one that goes right down the middle.

—Sandy Koufax

Control doesn't mean throwing strikes. It means throwing a pitch where you want it.

—Juan Marichal,
Hall of Fame pitcher
(1960–1975)

In pitching, as in real estate, there's a simple mantra: *Location, location, location.*

—Johnny Bench

The middle of the plate is where offensive history is written.

—Dan Quisenberry,
major-league pitcher
(1979–1990)

A pitcher's speed is worth nothing if he cannot put the ball where he wants to. To me, control is the first requirement of good pitching.

> —*Christy Mathewson,*
> *Hall of Fame pitcher*
> *(1900–1916)*

Generally, low pitches are most effective because the batter sees only the top half of the ball and cannot hit it squarely.

> —*Tom Seaver*

A mistake is a pitch I didn't execute well, one I left in an area where they could hit it. You don't call a ball a mistake because you miss the strike zone. . . . A mistake, to me, is a ball I leave in the middle of the plate.

> —*Orel Hershiser*

Show me a guy who can't pitch inside and I'll show you a loser.

> —*Sandy Koufax*

You pitch inside to make them [hitters] think inside, and then you get them outside.

> —*Bob Gibson,*
> *Hall of Fame pitcher*
> *(1959–1975)*

Throwing inside doesn't mean it has to be a strike. You pitch inside because you make your living outside. If you try to live away—even at 95 to 97 miles per hour—they're eventually going to get you. Even if the umpire doesn't give you the strike on a pitch two or three inches inside, it still sets up the hitter. It takes about an eighth of an inch of fear or doubt to keep him from hitting that fastball away. It takes that much doubt that you might come in again.

> —*Larry Andersen,*
> *major-league pitcher*
> *(1975–1994), broadcaster*

Pitching inside is essential. If you make the hitter conscious of the inside fastball, it sets up your pitches away.

> —*David Wells,*
> *major-league pitcher*
> *(1987–present)*

If a batter knows a pitcher will throw inside, he will be reluctant to dig in, and that's the edge the pitcher hoped he'd get.

—*Tim McCarver*

I used to pitch him outside a lot because I didn't want to hit him, and he just kept wearing me out. Finally, I got enough nerve to pitch him inside, though. I then started to have success with Joe DiMaggio.

—*Bob Feller*

A pitcher has to own the outside part of the plate to be successful.

—*Johnny Bench*

I rank location first. It tells the hitter you have command. Then movement. Only third comes velocity.

—*Andy Allanson,*
   major-league player
   (1986–1995)

MOVEMENT

I was taught that movement is more important than velocity. That advice came from somebody I trusted. I still believe that today.

—Greg Maddux

Throw as often as possible without overexerting. Make the ball do something without going to maximum effort.

—Leo Mazzone,
major-league coach
(1985, 1990–present)

The secret to pitching is to make your strikes look like balls and your balls look like strikes.

—Greg Maddux

VELOCITY

A pitcher needs very little power, provided he has control and uses his strength intelligently. Great speed is always prized and so is a sharp breaking curve. If these things go with good control and good judgment, they are immensely valuable, but by themselves they are worth very little. I would rather have a pitcher who has only moderate speed and a fair curve but knows how to use them.

—*Christy Mathewson*

Don't just throw once a day. Throwing a lot will help you build up arm strength and increase velocity better than any weight you can lift.

—*Leo Mazzone*

If I tried to throw the ball harder than I could, the ball went slower than it normally would.

—*Tom Seaver*

You don't just go out and throw a fastball 95 [mph] and win. . . . You have to know how to pitch.

—*Curt Schilling*

Speed is a decidedly bad qualification for pitching unless accuracy goes with it.

—*Cy Young,*
Hall of Fame pitcher
(1890–1911)

One of the best fastballs I'd ever thrown was hit for a home run [by the Braves' Joe Torre]. I learned the hard way that it would be impossible to get by in the major leagues with just a fastball, no matter how hard it was thrown.

—Nolan Ryan

My father once told me the harder you throw it, the less time you have to duck.

—Doug Jones,
major-league pitcher
(1982, 1986–present)

My dad and I played many hours of catch, even in the backyard between the outhouse and the house, and it gave me the encouragement I needed to believe in my abilities. I was always throwing, so that's probably why my arm was so strong.

—Bob Feller

I threw 78 miles per hour in high school. I hit 92 miles per hour during my freshman year in college, and today I can throw 98. If I can name one thing that contributed most to my increase in velocity, it would be long toss.

—Billy Wagner

The best way for a youngster to improve his fastball is just to throw it. I mean, just play catch all the time. Nothing takes the place of actually throwing.

> —*Mike Sheppard,*
> *college coach*

STRATEGY AND TACTICS

I became a good pitcher when I stopped trying to make them miss the ball and started trying to make them hit it.

> —*Sandy Koufax*

Pitching is essentially a sequential process that requires you to think like a hitter.

> —*Roger Craig,*
> *major-league pitcher*
> *(1955–1966), manager*

Every batter has a weakness. He may fight against it and refuse to admit it. He may even fail to recognize it as such. But it is there, and the pitcher's cue is to discover it and make the most of his discovery.

—*Ed Reulbach,*
major-league pitcher
(1905–1917)

First, it should be noted that successful pitchers do not *avoid* contact; neither do they *allow* contact. Successful pitchers *force* contact.

—*H. A. Dorfman,*
sports psychologist, author

In critical situations, I want our pitcher to go with his best pitch. Why would you want to get beat with your second-best pitch?

—*Davey Johnson,*
major-league player
(1965–1978), manager

If I'm facing a fastball hitter, I'm certainly not going to back down from throwing my best pitch. I mean, I have two different fastballs (a four-seam and a two-seam) that I can throw to different locations. So you can say it's power against power, but I still feel like I

own an advantage over the hitter because I can throw
the ball where I want. . . .

> —*Roger Clemens,*
> *major-league pitcher*
> *(1984–present)*

I try to throw the pitch that the hitter is least
expecting.

> —*Greg Maddux*

Anybody's best pitch is the one the batters ain't hitting
that day. And it doesn't take long to find out.

> —*Christy Mathewson*

A pitcher needs two pitches—one they're looking for
and one to cross 'em up.

> —*Warren Spahn,*
> *Hall of Fame pitcher*
> *(1942–1965)*

The most important pitch in the count for me is 1-1,
because 1-2 and 2-1 are two different worlds.

> —*Greg Maddux*

If I throw 100 pitches in a game, I'll probably throw as many as 70 fastballs. . . . Too many guys pitch backward. They throw their breaking ball so much that it's almost like their fastball is their off-speed pitch. What you have to realize is that a breaking ball is tough to throw for strikes. That means you have more pitchers pitching behind in the count, and that's when you get hit.

> —*Tom Glavine,*
> *major-league pitcher*
> *(1987–present)*

The strike-one count changes the complexion of an at-bat tremendously. It's on one pitch, but the hitter is behind in the count, and you can do a lot more things with your second pitch. You can expand the zone. . . .

> —*Mel Stottlemyre,*
> *major-league pitcher, coach*
> *(1984–present)*

What's the use of doin' in three pitches what you can do in one?

> —*Grover Cleveland Alexander,*
> *Hall of Fame pitcher*
> *(1911–1930)*

I exploit the greed of all hitters.

> —*Lew Burdette,*
> *major-league pitcher*
> *(1950–1967)*

When I get to 0-2 on a hitter, I like to get him out with the next pitch. I throw a lot of pitches as it is, I don't need to throw any extra ones.

> —*Bob Gibson*

If a man can beat you, walk him.

> —*Satchel Paige*

A man should always hold something in reserve, a surprise to spring when things get tight. If a pitcher has displayed his whole assortment to the batters early in the game and has used all his speed and his fastest breaking curve, then when the crisis comes he hasn't anything to fall back on.

> —*Christy Mathewson*

There are umpires that are pitchers' umpires and others that are hitters' umpires. What's important is that you throw to that particular umpire's strike zone—the one that is behind the plate that day. If you get frustrated with his zone, you're just going to hurt yourself.

—David Wells

CHANGING SPEEDS

Hitting is timing. Pitching is upsetting timing.

—Warren Spahn

A fastball helps the change-up, and the change-up helps the fastball.

—Tim McCarver

The real good pitchers are the guys who on 2-0 and 3-1 don't have to throw the fastball. They can get their change-up over, their slider, whatever.

—Whitey Herzog

No two pitches throughout the entire nine innings should come up to the plate at the same speed. . . . Don't let the batter get stepping in time with your rate of speed. If they step with you, they can hit the fastest thing you throw.

—Grover Cleveland Alexander

A curveball may bother an ordinary hitter, but if a man is a really good hitter, it's the old change-of-pace that causes him more trouble than all the freak deliveries in the world.

—Babe Ruth

A change-up thrown at the knees is 100 percent effective; a change-up thrown below the knees is 50 percent effective.

—Rod Dedeaux,
college coach

You have to remember that every good hitter is an egotist. If you can throw the fastball past them once, they'll make any adjustment to prevent it happening again. That makes the best of them gullible for a change-up.

—Warren Spahn

A change-up is not hard to learn. Long toss when you work on it. Once you warm up, play catch from about 100 feet away. Instead of throwing with your fastball grip, throw change-ups. That trains you to use the

same arm action as you would with a fastball. . . .
Allow your grip to do the work of slowing the ball
down.

> —*Mark Mulder,*
> *major-league pitcher*
> *(2000–present)*

Pitchers make the mistake of trying to underthrow
their change-ups, reducing their arm's speed to slow the
pitch. Throw the ball as if it were a fastball and let
your grip and motion do the work.

> —*Bill Lee,*
> *major-league pitcher*
> *(1969–1982)*

A curveball is not something you can pick up
overnight. It took me years to perfect mine.

> —*Bob Gibson*

The key element to throwing a good breaking ball is
getting the rotation, and you get that by applying
pressure to the seam with the middle finger.

> —*Mel Queen,*
> *major-league pitching coach*
> *(1982, 1996–1999)*

Sandy Koufax once told me that a so-so curveball
makes nine complete rotations on its way to home
plate. A good curveball rotates 11 times, and a great
curveball rotates 13 times. . . . The idea in throwing the
curveball is that, from the time the pitcher's arm
reaches the high point of his delivery until he releases
the ball, he creates so much pressure and so much snap
that the ball whooshes out of there with as much spin
as possible.

—Johnny Bench

Your goal as a pitcher is to change speeds and location.
A curveball does that all in one pitch.

—Aaron Sele,
major-league pitcher
(1993–present)

I can't tell you how many times in my career I've seen a
pitcher throw a good breaking ball for a strike and then
throw another one that gets crushed for a home run.
What happens is after throwing a good breaking ball,
pitchers will try to follow it with one that's even better.
More often than not, your accuracy suffers or you tense
up by trying to get too much break on the pitch. If
you've thrown a good curveball, the next doesn't
necessarily have to be thrown better.

—Dan Plesac

Proportionately, more home runs are hit on bad sliders than any other pitch. A "flat" slider, thrown with your fingers on the side of the ball rather than on top, lacks all of the Big Three pitch dimensions—velocity, movement, and location.

—*Tom Seaver*

Pitch selection is the most important and creative part of catching. When it's right, it's like the batter's a puppet. I decide what strings to pull, and the pitcher pulls them.

—*Carlton Fisk,*
Hall of Fame player
(1969–1993)

HOLDING RUNNERS

I'm licked when that pitcher takes the ball to his chest and just holds it there, just staring at you. You're tense out there on your toes, and this drains and kills your speed. Not all pitchers know that, though.

—*George Case,*
major-league player
(1937–1947)

When throwing to first, concentrate 100 percent on the runner, and when throwing to the plate, concentrate 100 percent on the batter. It's the 80 to 20 percent formula that will get you in trouble.

> —*Gene Mauch,*
> *major-league player, manager*
> *(1960–1982, 1985–1987)*

My approach for base stealers was to step on and off the rubber and try to break their timing of my delivery.

> —*Bob Feller*

MECHANICS

Don't try to copy your windup from some other pitcher. Find out what is comfortable for you. If someone were to give you a ball and tell you to go into your windup, 99 percent of the time that basic motion is what will serve you best because it's what is most natural for you.

> —*Bob Gibson*

You can have mechanics with no strategy, but without mechanics, there is no strategy.

—Orel Hershiser

Rushing is every pitcher's biggest nemesis. You are competitive and you want the ball to arrive at the plate quickly and deceptively. But don't make the mistake of thinking that the speed and power of your body will equate to the velocity and movement of the pitch. In fact, a rushed body without the proper timing leads to a lagging arm and ultimate injury—not the goals of your choice.

—Tom Seaver

Pitching is not being in a sport like boxing, football, or power lifting. It's a finesse skill. Any time you try to power the ball or call on your aggression as you can in other sports, your performance will suffer.

—Dan Plesac

Don't try to muscle the pitch to get greater velocity. When you tighten the arm to throw, it's like a hitter trying to hit a home run and swinging too hard. His bat gets very slow. The same thing will happen with

your arm. Keep your hand, wrist, and arm relaxed so
you can pop the ball at the very last second.

—Bob Gibson

Sound mechanics are so important in crucial game
situations. You can't be worrying about your delivery;
you still have to pitch and concentrate on what you
need to do to get the hitter. The last thing you want to
do is walk somebody in a tight spot because you're
thinking about your mechanics.

—David Wells

The follow-through is really important. That's what
saves your arm. Your muscles have to become fully
extended when you make a pitch. If you don't follow
through, or "finish," then you'll have recoil. . . . If you
recoil, you're playing with fire . . . risking injury.

—Pedro Martinez,
major-league pitcher
(1992–present)

Don't try to run before you can walk. Master the
simple things first (like controlling your fastball) before
jumping ahead to more advanced aspects of pitching.

—Dan Plesac

FIVE

FIELDING

If you don't catch the ball, you catch the bus.

> —*Rocky Bridges,*
> *major-league player*
> *(1951–1961)*

We should remember that with everything there is in the game of baseball, the thing there's most of are outs. That makes it pretty important to catch the ball and know what to do with it after you've caught it.

> —*Bill Rigney,*
> *major-league player*
> *(1946–1953), manager*

Championship baseball teams are not founded on bats.
They're built on a backbone of catching, pitching, a
second-base combination, and a centerfielder.

> —*Carl Mays,*
> *major-league pitcher*
> *(1915–1929)*

Be aggressive offensively—when in doubt, push. But
defensively, it's the opposite. Be very basic, take the outs
that are there, don't gamble in a way that will open up
a big inning for the other team.

> —*Tony La Russa,*
> *major-league player, manager*
> *(1979–present)*

You can have good defense without good pitching, but
you can't have good pitching without good defense.

> —*Earl Weaver*

Good defense in baseball is like good umpiring: It's
there, you expect it, but you don't really appreciate it.
But when it isn't there, then you notice it.

> —*Doug DeCinces,*
> *major-league player*
> *(1973–1987)*

Show me a great fielder and I'll show you a fielder who makes the routine play.

—*Mike Schmidt*

You can take 1,000 fungoes a day and it won't be as good as 10 minutes pretending you are in a game, taking balls off the bat during batting practice.

—*Tony La Russa*

INFIELD

It almost goes without saying that a confident infielder is a successful one. If you lack confidence as an infielder, your movements will be tentative and uncertain when the ball is hit in your direction.

—*Jerry Kindall*

Nobody has quick hands. To me, quick feet make quick hands. If you can move your feet quickly around the bag, your hands will move quicker at the same time.

—*Roberto Alomar*

A shortstop's job involves time. He has to field the ball and get to it first in a certain span of time, and most of them aren't creative enough to realize you can save time in other ways than with a strong arm. Get to the ball faster; get it off quicker. Ozzie [Smith] figured out early that you could save time these ways, too.

—*Whitey Herzog*

I can win a game with my glove just as easy as I can with my bat.

—*Keith Hernandez,*
major-league player
(1974–1990)

Never fake a throw during a rundown; you might fake out your teammate as well as the runner.

—*Joe Morgan*

There's no such thing as a bad hop. It's the way you played it.

—*Leo Durocher,*
major-league manager
(1939–1955, 1966–1973)

I like to learn their hitters and our pitchers and cheat a little bit, and cut down the area I have to cover. I'm not blessed with the kind of range a lot of shortstops have. The way I have success is, I guess, by thinking.

—*Cal Ripken Jr.*

My father, Sandy Alomar Sr., who played many years in the big leagues as an infielder, always taught me to play to my weaknesses. The toughest play for a second baseman is the backhand play, which is a ground ball to his right. The easiest play for a second baseman is a ball hit right at him or a ball to his left. So, if you position yourself a little more to your right, there will be less backhand territory to cover and the play up the middle can be made more easily.

—*Roberto Alomar*

More rallies have been killed by a skillful double-play combination at short and second than by any other defensive ingredient.

—*Jerry Kindall*

OUTFIELD

Don't get me wrong, I like to hit. But there's nothing like getting out there in the outfield, running after a ball, and throwing somebody out trying to take that extra base. That's real fun.

—*Willie Mays*

Now that I think of it, some of the best preparation for outfield might be playing infield.

—*Dick Howser,*
major-league player, manager
(1978, 1980–1986), coach

Throwing accuracy, especially from the outfield, is an underappreciated skill. The simple act of hitting the cutoff man or making a throw that can be easily handled by an infielder or catcher saves bases and runs, minimizing the damage already done by a ball hit to the outfield.

—*Dave Gallagher*

It's important to grip the ball with your fingers across the seams. A four-seam throw will keep the ball on a straight line through the air. The throw from the outfield is the longest throw on the field, so the straighter you can make the ball spin, the less chance it will have of cutting or fading away. Spin is very important.

> —*Brady Anderson,*
> *major-league player*
> *(1988–present)*

A lot of times the other team watches you—especially the third-base coach—and they'll see what you're throwing, and it will stay in their head. You want to plant that seed. Let them think about it so when the game comes, the runner peeks at you as he's going, the third-base coach's arms will somehow go up, stopping the runner. So you charge hard in practice and throw well—just as if it's in a game.

> —*Dwight Evans,*
> *major-league player*
> *(1972–1991)*

An outfielder who throws behind the runner is locking the barn after the horse was stolen.

> —*Joe McCarthy,*
> *Hall of Fame manager*
> *(1926–1946, 1948–1950)*

The phrase "off with the crack of the bat," while romantic, is really meaningless, since the outfielder should be in motion long before he hears the sound of the ball meeting the bat.

—Joe DiMaggio

Getting a good jump on the ball starts at home plate. You have to know who is hitting. If you don't know where the hitter tends to hit the ball, how can you get a good jump on it?

—Willie Mays

Catch every [fly] ball in as close to the ideal position as possible. If you drift, a sudden gust of wind, a slight stumble, or a ball hit harder than you expected will make a difficult play out of what should have been a routine catch.

—Jerry Kindall

When you are going into the gap, don't keep your eyes on the ball. Train yourself to recognize where the ball will probably land and run to that area. After four or five steps, you can glance up to check the flight of the ball.

—Ken Griffey Sr.,
major-league player
(1973–1991), coach

CATCHING

Look, I like hitting fourth and I like the good batting average. But what I do every day behind the plate is a lot more important because it touches so many more people and so many more aspects of the game.

> —*Thurman Munson,*
> *major-league player*
> *(1969–1979)*

THE FIELD GENERAL

Catching is much like managing. Managers don't really win games, but they can lose plenty of them. The same way with catching. If you're doing a quality job, you should be anonymous.

> —*Bob Boone,*
> *major-league player*
> *(1972–1990), manager*

A good catcher is the quarterback, the carburetor, the lead dog, the pulse taker, the traffic cop. . . . No team gets very far without one.

> —*Miller Huggins,*
> *major-league player,*
> *Hall of Fame manager*
> *(1913–1929)*

Does the man [catcher] back there know what's going on? If he does, he can throw bad and he can run bad and block bad, but he's still the single most important player on the field.

> —*Ted Simmons,*
> *major-league player*
> *(1968–1988)*

Very few things happen on a major-league baseball field by chance. Every pitch, every swing of the bat, every throw is made with specific intention. And at the center of everything that happens is the catcher.

> —*Ron Luciano,*
> *major-league umpire*
> *(1968–1980)*

TECHNIQUE

There are a few little tricks of framing and catching the ball that might convince an umpire [the pitch is a strike]—shifting your body instead of your glove, or maybe the way you collapse your glove as you make the catch. . . . More often a catcher will take a strike away from the pitcher by catching it improperly—knocking it out of the strike zone, or moving the glove with the pitch so that it carries the ball out of the strike zone after the catch, and even if you roll your glove you might help the umpire to make up his mind the wrong way.

—Bob Boone

Now, to block the plate, a lot of catchers think they have to be squarely in front of it. Well, if you're blocking the plate from the time that ball's hit, a runner coming around third base can't see home plate. He has two choices: Go around you and try to come back and touch his hand on the plate, or go right through you. The mentality of most runners is to run over you. So I learned to let that runner see home plate. . . . I wanted him on the ground, not in the air, banging into my shoulder.

—Johnny Bench

Framing is not pulling bad pitches into the strike zone and hoping to fool the umpire; that practice rarely works and serves only to alienate the umpire. Framing is used to ensure that pitches on the edge of the strike zone will indeed be called strikes.

—Jerry Kindall

If a catcher can't block a tough pitch in the dirt with a runner on third in a one-run game, the pitcher can't let his best curveball or split-finger go for fear it will end up at the screen. You'd be surprised how many times during the season a pitcher gets blamed for hanging a curveball or split-finger, and the reason he hangs it is because he's afraid his catcher won't catch the tough one.

—*Tim McCarver*

When people talk about throwing out base runners, they are almost always thinking about arms, but they should be thinking about feet. A catcher has to have quick feet so he can he can "get under himself" and move fluidly from a receiving position to a throwing position. Your feet will get your shoulders turned and in position to throw.

—*Johnny Bench*

BEFORE THE BALL IS PITCHED

When you have a lead, and one out is enough, you can play a deeper double-play depth. Perhaps you will miss a double play you might have had playing at the regular depth, but you will get to some balls you might not have reached at regular double-play depth. And you cut the trailing team from nine down to eight outs remaining. Similarly, when you absolutely must have a double play—say, tie game, eighth inning, one out, runners on first and second, fast runner at the plate—there is a shallower-than-usual double-play depth.

> —*Cal Ripken Jr.*

I take two steps forward and get into a bent-knee position, balanced on the balls of my feet, ready to go on every pitch. I believe it's important to anticipate that the ball is going to be hit my way on every pitch.

> —*Ryne Sandberg,*
> *major-league player*
> *(1981–1994, 1996–1997)*

Catching a fly ball is pleasure, but knowing what to do with it after you catch it is a business.

> —*Tommy Henrich,*
> *major-league player*
> *(1937–1950)*

Outfield positioning is more important than infield positioning because outfielders have much more room to cover.

> —*Tim McCarver*

Outfield positioning is a product of many factors: knowing the hitter's tendencies, playing to the count, reading the location of the pitch, and being in motion as the pitch reaches the hitting zone, among others. Good outfield positioning can and does help a player with only average foot speed cover the same amount of ground as a very fast outfielder.

—Dave Gallagher

Pitch selection is the most important and creative part of catching. When it's right, it's like the batter's a puppet. I decide what strings to pull, and the pitcher pulls them.

—Carlton Fisk

The thing that isn't looked at is, how many [runners] do you deter from running? The great base runners are going to steal bases, but you eliminate the other guys from even attempting to steal.

—Johnny Bench

The thing about a pickoff play is not just the 26 or 27 guys you get a year—and I don't want to minimize that—but it just kills a ball club. It happens to us every

once in a while, and you can just feel the whole club go
flat.

—Ray Miller

A pitchout is an important part of defense. If I go
against a team that doesn't pitch out on us, it's just like
getting a free pass—run anytime you want.

—Tony La Russa

SIX

BASERUNNING

Cool Papa's [James Bell] so fast he can turn off the light and be in bed before the room gets dark.

—Satchel Paige

They say baseball is a game of inches. Well, there are plenty of inches you can gain on the base paths if you know where to find them.

—Ron Plaza,
major-league coach
(1978–1983, 1986)

The most aggressive thing in baseball is guys on base running around and sliding, raising dust.

—Tony La Russa

Speed is a great asset, but it's greater when it's combined with quickness—and there's a big difference.

—*Ty Cobb*

Baserunning is a skill so often overlooked in baseball. . . . Good baserunning—or bad baserunning—will win or lose more games for you than any other aspect of the game.

—*Don Zimmer,*
major-league player,
manager (1972–1973,
1976–1982, 1988–1991),
coach

Baserunning arrogance is just like pitching arrogance or hitting arrogance. You are a force, and you have to instill you are a force in the opposition.

—*Lou Brock*

Effective running requires good technique from every muscle in your body. A swimming coach would never tell his team, "Forget technique. Just get from one end of the pool to the other as fast you can."

—*Jerry Kindall*

Many players are thrown out by a split second. When you hit the ball, run it out with all the speed you have, no matter where or how you hit it. This, I claim, will earn you many hits during the season that you would not get otherwise.

—*Ty Cobb*

TAKING THE EXTRA BASE

Good base runners only need a coach to stop them. Bad base runners need a coach to make them go.

—*Dave Gallagher*

Take that extra base every time. Make them throw after you; make them hurry their throws. You'll get thrown out for sure, but for every time they throw you out now, you will make them hurry and throw wild later. You will reap a golden harvest of extra bases.

—*Branch Rickey*

My philosophy is to do anything you can to make the other team nervous. A running team puts a lot of pressure on the other side. You pressure the catcher, obviously. But, in addition, you put a lot of heat on the

infield. . . . It's a funny thing. Running brings your
team together—and also brings the crowd to its feet.

> —*Davey Lopes,*
> *major-league player*
> *(1972–1987), manager*

There are 26 ways to score from third base. Get there!

> —*Gordie Gillespie,*
> *college coach*

It's just as important to know when not to go as it is to
know when to go.

> —*Maury Wills,*
> *Hall of Fame player*
> *(1959–1972), manager*

Pete Rose was one of the best base runners I ever
played with or against. From the stands, Pete appeared
to be fast because he hustled all the time, but he only
had average speed. . . . Pete went from first to third as
well as any player in the majors because of his head,
not his legs. He always knew where the ball was hit and
the strength of the outfielder's arm.

> —*Joe Morgan*

You run through the base, not to the base, to give yourself a chance to take an extra base.

> —*Eddie Stanky,*
> *major-league player*
> *(1943–1953), manager*

Slide head first at second or third base if you must, but for me, it's off limits at first or home. The risk of injury is not worth the reward.

> —*Dave Gallagher*

STEALING BASES

A good base stealer should make the whole infield jumpy. Whether you steal or not, you're changing the rhythm of the game. If the pitcher is concerned about you, he isn't concentrating enough on the batter.

> —*Joe Morgan*

When you steal a base, 99 percent of the time you steal on a pitcher. You actually never steal on a catcher. In order to be a good base stealer, you must study the mechanics of the pitcher's style—how he delivers it to the hitter. Most important, you have to run when you get your best jump. . . .

—*Lou Brock*

Stealing bases was something I had to learn to do when I came up to the majors. I had to learn how to read pitchers, look for habits and tendencies.

—*Tony Gwynn*

A guy who gets on base and is a threat to steal can be just as important to a lineup, if not more so, than a power hitter. Not only is he capable of getting himself into scoring position by swiping a base, but he is also a distraction to the pitcher, catcher, and infield defense. And any time the pitcher is not 100 percent focused on the player at the plate, he's more apt to make a mistake, which gives your teammate at bat (and your team) a distinct advantage.

—*Maury Wills*

SEVEN

MANAGING AND COACHING

I've always gone back to the belief that you don't win—
that the other team usually beats itself. That's why I'll
continue to emphasize pitching and defense. You get
those two things straightened out and the offense will
take care of itself.

> —*Dick Williams,*
> *major-league player, manager*
> *(1967–1969, 1971–1988)*

Most one-run games are lost, not won.

> —*Gene Mauch*

Your most precious possessions on offense are your 27 outs.

     —Earl Weaver

If you play for one run, that's all you'll get.

     —Earl Weaver

I don't like them fellas who drive in two runs and let in three.

     —Casey Stengel,
      major-league player, manager
      (1934–1965)

You don't save a pitcher for tomorrow. Tomorrow it may rain.

     —Leo Durocher

MANAGING

In baseball you take nothing for granted. You look after all the little details, or suddenly this game will kick you right in the butt.

     —Jim Lefebvre

You can't sit on a lead and run a few plays into the line and just kill the clock. You've got to throw the ball over the plate and give the other man his chance. That's why baseball is the greatest game of them all.

—Earl Weaver

You have to take the pulse of your players, so you know who needs in-depth personal attention and who doesn't, who needs coaching and who doesn't, who needs a private dialogue with you and who doesn't, who you can count on in tough spots and who you can't. To develop this level of knowledge about your team players, you need some insight into their personal and emotional qualities.

—Joe Torre,
major-league player, manager
(1977–1984, 1990–present)

Mr. Torre never panics and he always stays positive. That's why the Yankees continue to make it to the postseason.

—Derek Jeter

Managing is simple. You pick out your best players and try to get them out there in their positions as often as possible.

—Whitey Herzog

I play my best nine, not my nine best.

>—*Skip Bertman,*
>*college coach*

. . . so many managers forget they were players
themselves. To respect your ballplayers is the main
thing. The problem of managing is human relations.

>—*Orlando Cepeda,*
>*Hall of Fame player*
>*(1958–1974)*

Managers can't be afraid of criticism. No one ever wins
anything by playing it safe.

>—*Sparky Anderson,*
>*major-league manager*
>*(1970–1995)*

The best game managers, generally speaking, are those
who have the courage to keep their hands in their
pockets, let their players play. . . . A strategic move or
two a game is OK, but those guys who are out there
pulling levers and pushing buttons like they were
playing some super-advanced version of Donkey Kong

are probably giving away more on balance than they are getting back.

—Bill James,
baseball historian, author

Grant them [assistants] full authority in their area of expertise. Trust that they will get everything done exactly as you discussed it. Don't be checking up on them in the field. Never second-guess anyone. If your third-base coach sends in a runner and the player is thrown out by 20 feet, don't say a word. In 26 years, I never questioned any of my third-base coach's decisions.

—Sparky Anderson

You hear about those utility players who play very little but are content with their role on the club. I love those guys—as long as they are on someone else's club. I never wanted anyone on my roster who was happy about not playing. You want guys who want to be out on the field, so that when you give them a chance, they're going to bring some fire to the lineup.

—Sparky Anderson

The night we won the World Series, I was understandably feeling my oats. I asked my wife how many really great managers she thought there were in baseball. Glaring at me, she said, "I think there's one less than you do."

> —*Danny Murtaugh,*
> *major-league player, manager*
> *(1957–1976)*

If you don't make any promises to your players, you won't have to break them.

> —*Earl Weaver*

Games are won by a combination of informed aggression and prudence based on information.

> —*George Will*

Communication is the key to trust, and trust is the key to teamwork in any endeavor, be it sports, business, or family.

> —*Joe Torre*

There are three secrets to managing. The first secret is "have patience." The second is "be patient." And the third most important secret is "patience."

> —*Chuck Tanner,*
> *major-league player, manager*
> *(1970–1988)*

I'm not buddy-buddy with the players. If they need a buddy, let them buy a dog.

—*Whitey Herzog*

I'd yank my own son if it was the right move.

—*Eddie Stanky*

All I've tried to do as a manager of this team is to get the fear of losing the hell out of this clubhouse.

—*Felipe Alou,*
major-league player, manager
(1992–2000)

I can't understand it when I hear a manager say something like, "We've got to have a leader on this club." What are you paying the manager for? If you need a leader, then fire the manager and get somebody else.

—*Cal Ripken Sr.*

Run production is how you measure hitters. Wins and losses are how you measure pitchers. Batting averages and ERAs are personal stats.

—*Joe Morgan*

All [Earl] Weaver understood about the curveball is that he couldn't hit one. So that's what he wanted you to throw.

> —*Jim Palmer,*
> *Hall of Fame pitcher*
> *(1965–1984)*

COACHING

Coaches don't win games. They prepare players to win games.

> —*Dick Williams*

Tell a ballplayer something a thousand times, then tell him again, because that might be the time he'll understand something.

> —*Paul Richards,*
> *major-league manager*
> *(1951–1961, 1976)*

A good teacher needs his students, and you can't solve the problem by raising your voice. The guys who need to hear you—you'll only turn them off that way.

> —*Whitey Herzog*

If you ignore it, that means you have accepted it.

> —*Ron Oestrike, college coach*

You have no idea the pressure a young pitcher is under. I've walked out to the mound in the middle of an inning and the pitcher couldn't tell me his telephone number. By walking out, you calm him down. . . . Yelling at a boy from the bench is confusing and ridiculous.

> —*Johnny Sain,*
> *major-league pitcher*
> *(1942–1955), coach*

Players may swing the bat the same and have the same speed, but they're different! You have to recognize you're dealing with different personalities.

> —*Jim Leyland,*
> *major-league manager*
> *(1986–1999)*

Any coach can make his players more comfortable by letting them know that some failure is inevitable, that it's all right to make some mistakes. Good coaches are not as much disappointed *in* their players for failing as they are disappointed *for* them. That gives players a level of comfort necessary for rebounding from failure.

—*Dave Gallagher*

Remember, coaches, you're not coaching baseball. You are coaching people.

—*Bill Arce,*
college coach

The hitters will tell you [the pitcher] when you're through.

—*Ray Ripplemeyer,*
major-league pitcher, coach
(1970–1978)

I have long believed that pitching is notoriously undercoached, that kids are taught to throw as hard as they can, being obsessed with radar speeds rather than learning what makes their ball move from one side of the plate to the other and how to improve their control.

—*Skip Bertman*

I want my guys to look like they're stealing on every pitch, because if you're playing someone like La Russa and you do one little thing different [when you are ready to steal], he's going to pitch out.

—Jim Leyland

Make your practices like games. Make your games like practices.

—John Herbold, college coach

EIGHT

CHARACTER

You gotta believe!

>—*Tug McGraw,*
>*major-league pitcher*
>*(1965–1984)*

Be on time. Bust your butt. Play smart. And have some laughs while you're at it.

>—*Whitey Herzog*

There is always some kid who may be seeing me for the first or last time. I owe him my best.

>—*Joe DiMaggio*

Success in baseball requires the synthesis of a great many virtues, many of which have nothing to do with sheer talent. Self-discipline, single-mindedness, perseverance, ambition—these were all virtues I was positive I possessed . . . but which I've discovered over the years I did not.

—Pat Jordan,
author, minor-league pitcher

PREPARATION

Luck is the residue of design.

—Branch Rickey

As a boy in Kalamazoo, I lived for game day. When the season would start, I would put my uniform on and ask my parents how I looked. I loved the whole ritual of game day: putting on my uniform, driving to the field, doing our warm-ups, hearing the crowd cheer and my name called, and taking my place at shortstop. It's a thrilling memory and one that I relive every time I put on a Yankee uniform today.

—Derek Jeter

TEAMWORK

A team is where a boy can prove his courage on his own. A gang is where a coward goes to hide.

—*Mickey Mantle,*
Hall of Fame player
(1951–1968)

I'm proud of all my stats, but I don't think I ever got one for Joe Morgan. If I stole a base, it was to help us win a game, and I like to think that's what made me a little special.

—*Joe Morgan*

The difference between the old ballplayer and the new ballplayer is the jersey. The old ballplayer cared about the name on the front. The new ballplayer cares about the name on the back.

—*Steve Garvey,*
major-league player
(1969–1987)

A selfish player is someone who goes for the RBI when he should be trying to move runners over, or steals in a nonstealing situation to pad his stats, or gives up a leadoff triple with a four-run lead and then goes for strikeouts instead of giving up a run for an out. He's also the guy who lets his offense affect his defense and vice versa.

—*Orel Hershiser*

I wanted to win this game [Game 7 of the 1995 World Series, in which he was taken out after eight shutout innings] as badly as any in my life, but I felt I had to fight my emotions and keep my ego in check.

—*Tom Glavine*

POTENTIAL

Nothing is more common than unsuccessful men with talent.

—*Charlie Lau*

The difference between the possible and the impossible lies in the man's determination.

—*Tommy Lasorda,*
major-league manager
(1976–1996)

Baseball is no place for a lazy man. A player must first
of all have ability. But ability is not enough. He must
have ambition, for unless he strives to succeed he will
not succeed. Ambition means hard work.

—Jake Daubert

COURAGE

Show me a guy who's afraid to look bad, and I'll show
you a guy you can beat every time.

—Lou Brock

The great [pitchers] are all competitors—they can
hardly wait to get into the game. They fight you like
hell when you try to get them off.

—Sparky Anderson

The first great requisite for success in baseball is nerve.
I have seen players with speed, hitting, strength, and
grace, but they did not make good. They lack the
prime essential, stoutness of heart.

—Bill Carrigan,
major-league manager
(1913–1916, 1927–1929)

Jeter surpasses expectations, partly because he's not afraid to make a mistake, to embarrass himself. He'll often grab a ground ball deep in the hole between short and third, twist his body in midair, and while still airborne, whip a perfect throw to first base that beats the runner in a photo finish. I've seen him blow that play, but usually he succeeds. . . . A player like Derek Jeter will be more successful because he's not afraid to make a mistake.

—Joe Torre

A big player has to prove he can't play; a little one has to prove that he can.

—Len Merullo,
major-league scout

I would take the chance to be the hero or goat in every game I play for the rest of my life. Those moments are what make playing sports so exhilarating, whether it's a last-second shot, a field goal as time expires, or a 3-2 count with two outs and the winning run on base in the ninth inning. . . . To me, that's fun.

—Derek Jeter

BE YOURSELF

Baseball is both the greatest and worst thing that ever happened to me. Not because people asked too much of me, but because I asked too much of myself. As it turned out, my talent was a curse. The curse was the way I handled it and didn't handle it.

> —*Sam McDowell,*
> *major-league pitcher*
> *(1961–1975)*

Smiling and waving is just not me.

> —*Barry Bonds,*
> *major-league player*
> *(1986–present)*

I don't want to be a hero; I don't want to be a star. It just works out that way.

> —*Reggie Jackson*

LEADERSHIP

Having Willie Stargell on your team is like having a
diamond ring on your finger.

—Chuck Tanner

A good team leader is one who takes a little more than
his share of the blame and a little less than his share of
the credit.

—Reggie Jackson

BEING A WINNER

We didn't think he [Jackie Robinson] was the best. He
ran well and he was a fighter, but he wasn't one of the
Negro "stars." It just goes to show that you can't always
tell about a ballplayer. Branch Rickey saw something
there and he was right. Robinson was the man for the
job—college-educated, a winner, a man with good self-
control.

—Buck Leonard,
Negro League player
(1933–1950)

He looked like he was falling apart when he ran. [He] looked like he was coming apart when he threw. His stance at the plate was ridiculous. When he swung, he'd lunge and hit bad balls. There was no way he could hit the ball like that. But no one told Roberto [Clemente] that.

—*Robin Roberts,*
major-league pitcher
(1948–1966)

The spirit to win is worth 20 points to any batting average and an additional pitcher to any club.

—*Fred Mitchell,*
major-league player, manager
(1917–1923)

I'm an aggressive player. I'll do anything to win.

—*George Brett*

HUSTLE

Let me tell you about running out everything. Back in the 1960s, Ray Washburn of the Cardinals was beating us 7–0 late in the game. With two outs, I hit a one-hopper right back to him. I kept running and he threw the ball high to first base, and by the time Bill White came down with the ball, I was safe. By the end of that inning, we had an 8–7 lead.

—*Pete Rose*

You ought to run the hardest when you feel the worst.

—*Joe DiMaggio*

Does he [Pete Rose] hustle? Before the All-Star game he came into the clubhouse and took off his shoes— and they ran another mile without him.

—*Hank Aaron,*
Hall of Fame player
(1954–1976)

DEALING WITH FAILURE

What differentiates the better players from the rest is how they cope with temporary failure, no matter how exceedingly frustrating it is.

—*Rod Carew*

I don't understand why players who make a mistake—
boot a ball, strike out, or give up a key hit—throw
helmets, bats, or fits. All that does is draw attention to
how poorly they are performing. Better to behave as
you do when you're playing well, so that your failures
are less noticeable.

—*Dave Gallagher*

I'm not perfect. I have made errors that have caused us
to lose games. I have dropped balls, struck out with
men on base, been caught stealing to end a rally. The
best players fail at times. But I look at the balls I catch,
not the ones I miss, and I savor the game-winning hits
and try not to worry about the strikeouts.

—*Derek Jeter*

About the only problem with success is that it does not
teach you how to deal with failure.

—*Tommy Lasorda*

BIBLIOGRAPHY

BOOKS

Altopp, David (ed.). *Coach Quotes for Baseball*. Monterey, CA: Coaches Choice, 2000.

Angell, Roger. *Season Ticket: A Baseball Companion*. Boston: Houghton Mifflin, 1988.

Bench, Johnny. *The Complete Idiot's Guide to Baseball*. New York: Alpha, 1999.

Boggs, Wade. *The Techniques of Modern Hitting*. New York: Putnam, 1990.

Carew, Rod. *The Art and Science of Hitting*. New York: Penguin Books, 1986.

Curran, William. *A Celebration of the Art of Pitching*. New York: Crown, 1995.

Dickson, Paul (ed.). *Baseball's Greatest Quotations*. New York: HarperCollins, 1991.

DiMaggio, Joe. *Baseball for Everyone*. New York: Whittlesey House, 1948.

Dorfman, H. A. *The Mental ABC's of Pitching*. South Bend, IN: Diamond Communications, 2000.

———. *The Mental Game of Baseball*. South Bend, IN: Diamond Communications, 1998.

———. *The Mental Keys to Hitting*. South Bend, IN: Diamond Communications, 2001.

Falkner, David. *Nine Sides of the Diamond*. New York: Random House, 1990.

From the Archives of the Sporting News: 100 Years of the Modern Era 1901–2000. St. Louis: The Sporting News, 2001.

Gola, Mark, and John Monteleone. *The Louisville Slugger® Complete Book of Hitting Faults and Fixes*. Chicago: Contemporary Books, 2001.

———. *The Louisville Slugger® Ultimate Book of Hitting*. New York: Henry Holt, 1997.

Gola, Mark, and Doug Myers. *The Louisville Slugger® Complete Book of Pitching*. Chicago: Contemporary Books, 2000.

Gwynn, Tony, with Roger Vaughan. *The Art of Hitting*. New York: GT Publishing, 1998.

Herzog, Whitey. *You're Missing a Perfect Game*. New York: Simon & Schuster, 1999.

Kahn, Roger. *The Head Game: Baseball Seen from the Pitcher's Mound*. New York: Harcourt, 2000.

Koppett, Leonard. *The New Thinking Fan's Guide to Baseball*. New York: Simon & Schuster, 1991.

Krasner, Steven. *Play Ball Like the Pros*. Atlanta: Peachtree, 2002.

Lane, F. C. *Batting*. Cleveland, OH: Society for American Baseball Research, 2001.

Lau, Charley. *The Art of Hitting .300*. New York: Hawthorn, 1980.

Leonard, Bernardo, and Peter Golenbock. *The Superstar Hitter's Bible*. Chicago: Contemporary Books, 1998.

Mazzone, Leo, and Jim Rosenthal. *Pitch Like a Pro*. New York: St. Martin's Press, 1999.

McCarver, Tim, and Danny Peary. *Tim McCarver's Baseball for Brain Surgeons and Other Fans*. New York: Villard Books, 1998.

Morgan, Joe, with Richard Lally. *Baseball for Dummies*, 2nd ed. Foster City, CA: IDG Books Worldwide, 2000.

Ripken, Cal, Sr. *The Ripken Way*. New York: Pocket Books, 1999.

Rubin, Louis D. *The Quotable Baseball Fanatic*. New York: Lyons Press, 2000.

Schmidt, Mike, and Rob Ellis. *The Mike Schmidt Study*. Atlanta: McGriff and Bell, 1994.

Seaver, Tom. *The Art of Pitching*. New York: Hearst, 1984.

Thorn, John (ed.). *Total Baseball*, 7th ed. New York: Total Sports, 2001.

Torre, Joe, with Henry Dreher. *Joe Torre's Grand Rules for Winners*. New York: Hyperion, 1999.

Weaver, Earl. *Weaver on Strategy*. New York: Macmillan, 1984.

Will, George F. *Bunts*. New York: Simon & Schuster, 1998.

———. *Men at Work*. New York: Macmillan, 1990.

Williams, Ted. *The Science of Hitting*. New York: Simon & Schuster, 1970.

MAGAZINES

The Sporting News. July 11, 1994, June 5, 1995, August 3, 1998.

Sports Illustrated. May 2, 1988, May 1, 1995, April 1, 1996, March 31, 1997, July 28, 1997, May 4, 1998, September 4, 2000, June 4, 2001, March 25, 2002, June 24, 2002.

Sports Illustrated for Kids. June 1, 2002.

NEWSPAPERS

Dallas Morning News. June 3, 1998.

WEBSITES

Baseball-almanac.com
Bemorecreative.com

INDEX